Discovering
Life in
Christ

Student

Joseph Miller

Regular Baptist Press
1300 North Meacham Road
Schaumburg, Illinois 60173–4888

REGULAR BAPTIST PRESS
1300 North Meacham Road
Schaumburg, Illinois 60173–4888

In Canada: Regular Baptist Press Canada, 1564 Hillside Drive, London, Ontario
N6G 4M6

STUDENT
© 1989, Regular Baptist Press. Printed in U.S.A.
Vernon D. Miller, Executive Editor; Norman A. Olson, Book
Editor; Jonita Barram, Assistant; Pat Carapelle, Assistant; Cover
Design, Joe Ragont; Graphic Arts, John Shafer

Second printing—1992

Contents

About the Author

Joseph Miller, who is a graduate of the Moody Bible Institute Pastor's Course and received a B.R.E. degree from Grand Rapids Baptist College, has a varied background in Christian education and the pastorate. He has served as a minister of education, a Bible college instructor and administrator, a church-planter and a pastor. He has also written for the *Baptist Bulletin* and for the Sunday School Curriculum Department of Regular Baptist Press. Currently he serves as a church ministries consultant and as editor of the *Church Planter*. Miller and his wife, Helen, have four grown children.

How to Use This Book

The questions have been numbered consecutively throughout each lesson; they appear in bold type to make them easier to find. The answers are on pages 70–76.

Discovering Life in Christ is designed to be used in a variety of ways. If you are using the book as

• **a self-study,** read the passage at the beginning of each chapter and memorize the verses. Then read the lesson, answering the questions in the spaces provided. Each main section closes with a list of principles to practice. You can apply the lesson to your life by doing the suggested activities.

• **a one-on-one discipleship guide,** read the lesson, answer the questions and check your answers before you meet with your discipler. When you meet with him, he can answer any questions you have concerning the lesson, discuss some topics in depth and suggest further activities to help you apply the lesson.* After your meeting, follow the Principles to Practice.

• **a class situation (church membership class, small study group or alternative to regular Sunday School curriculum),** read the lesson, answer the questions and check your answers before you go to your study group. During the study, your leader will answer your questions, discuss related topics and suggest further activities to help you apply the lesson.* After class follow the Principles to Practice.

*Take a notebook to your study or class so you can take notes, answer questions and make plans.

Lesson 1

The Believer and the Book

Passage to Read: Psalm 119:1–24

1. List the different names for God's Word, the condition and the blessing.

Verses	Name	Condition	Blessing

2. List the words that tell what a Christian should do with God's Word. _____

_____

_____

Passage to Memorize: 2 Timothy 2:15
(Suggestion: Write the verse on a 3 x 5 card that you can carry with you. Study it during the times that you have to wait for something or while you jog, etc.)

Introduction

The newborn infant requires proper nourishment, exercise and rest in order to mature and to enjoy physical health. The caring parents follow the instructions of doctors, books and "experts" on child care. The plan for feeding progresses from milk to cereal, to strained foods and finally to meat and other table foods according to the maturity level of the child's system, which can now digest the solid food.

Now that we are older, few of us miss a meal. We are concerned that others as well as ourselves get proper physical nourishment and exercise. We want to be healthy, look healthy and feel healthy. We live in an era of great emphasis on physical fitness: "How's your weight? Are you watching the junk foods? Have you been keeping up with your exercise program?"

In the spiritual realm, life in Christ is described as "the new birth"—to be born of the Spirit of God. The infant in Christ must then have the proper spiritual nourishment, exercise and rest in order to develop spiritual maturity and to enjoy the abundant life that Christ came to provide (John 10:10).

God has given us the Bible to nourish us in order to have spiritual vitality. Let's notice the Bible's provisions for us.

New Life

"In whom ye also trusted, after that ye heard the word of truth, the gospel of your salvation: in whom also after that ye believed, ye were sealed with that holy Spirit of promise" (Ephesians 1:13). We children of God were born into His family through the ministry of His Word. The Holy Spirit used the Bible to convince us that we are sinners and to convict us of our sins (Romans 3:23).

Faith in God is the result of hearing the Word of God. In like manner, faith increases by a greater knowledge of the Word. "So then faith cometh by hearing, and hearing by the word of God" (Romans 10:17).

The Spirit of God used the Word to convict us of rebellion against Christ, Who died for our sins. First, we saw our lack of righteousness (or rightness) compared to the sinless character of Christ. Second, we learned through the Bible that retribution, or punishment, for our sin was inevitable (John 16:8–11).

This eternal life that we now possess was conceived by the Spirit of God through the Word. "Jesus answered and said unto him, Verily, verily, I say unto thee, Except a man be born again, he cannot see the kingdom of God. . . . Except a man be born of water [cleansing] and of the Spirit, he cannot enter into the kingdom of God" (John 3:3, 5).

This "born again" comes by the Spirit, Who imparts new life through the Word of God, based upon the satisfaction that Christ provided when He died for our sins. "Who his own self bare our sins in his own body on the tree, that we, being dead to sins, should live unto righteousness: by whose stripes ye were healed" (1 Peter 2:24).

It is the Word of God that provides the spiritual cleansing to remove the stain of sin and make us children of God. In John 15:3 Christ announced, "Now ye are clean through the word which I have spoken unto you."

In addition to conception and cleansing, proper care is essential to the child's existence and proper development. This is also true of the spiritual child of God. The Holy Spirit uses the Word to care for us and to give us the sense of security that is essential for proper child development.

It is the Word of God that teaches us life is eternal. "And this is the record, that God hath given to us eternal life, and this life is in his Son. He that hath the Son hath life; and he that hath not the Son of God hath not life. These things have I written unto you that believe on the name of the Son of God; that ye may know that ye have eternal life, and that ye may believe on the name of the Son of God" (1 John 5:11–13).

Eternal security, or always remaining God's children, depends upon God. Assurance of this security, or feeling secure, depends upon our knowing what God's Word says, believing it and obeying it. We are not going to feel saved if we do not feed on God's Word and obey its instructions. "The Spirit itself beareth witness with our spirit, that we are the children of God" (Rom. 8:16).

State in your own words the plan of salvation that you followed to become a child of God. _____

_____

_____

_____

_____

_____

_____

New Look

Spiritual babes, who were born of the Word of God, must feed on God's Word to develop spiritually. We are commanded to study the Bible as a means of gaining God's approval. "Study to shew thyself approved unto God, a workman that needeth not to be ashamed, rightly dividing the word of truth" (2 Timothy 2:15).

The Bible provides the nourishing milk needed by babes in Christ (1 Peter 2:2). Normal spiritual growth results in the ability to understand deeper truths of the Word as we develop spiritually (Hebrews 5:14).

This text teaches us that it is normal to grow in our new life and to develop a new look. Spiritual training (exercise), which comes through Bible study and practice, leads to healthy, mature spiritual life, which in turn brings the new look of the abundant life in Christ (2 Corinthians 5:17).

The Spirit of God will use the Word of God to continue convicting us so that we will develop the new look. We'll be changed. "For the word of God is quick, and powerful, and sharper than any twoedged sword, piercing even to the dividing asunder of soul and spirit, and of the joints and marrow, and is a discerner of the thoughts and intents of the heart" (Hebrews 4:12).

The Word of God has the ability to develop new life through the new nature that we received when we were born into God's family. The term "quick" in the verse above means "life-giving." As we feed our new nature the Word of God, our new life becomes evident in our new look. We gain the ability to put off the old life and to put on the new. Furthermore, the new look is not merely different, it is also clean.

The Bible will continue to work as a cleanser of our lives. "Wherewithal shall a young man cleanse his way? by taking heed thereto according to thy word" (Psalm 119:9). We cannot change ourselves; our old lives will be replaced with the new look of the new life when we study and practice God's Word.

The Holy Spirit came to live in each of us at the moment we received Christ as our personal Savior. He is the author of the Bible and the personal tutor of each believer to instruct us in God's Word as we study and obey it (1 Corinthians 2:14; 6:19, 20). When we obey God's Word, the Holy Spirit ministers to us to guide us in understanding what to believe as well as how to behave.

The Holy Spirit also produces spiritual fruit in our lives—fruit of a new look. "But the fruit of the Spirit is love, joy, peace, longsuffering, gentleness, goodness, faith, meekness, temperance: against such there is no law" (Galatians 5:22, 23). This cluster of the characteristics of our new life is progressive, beginning with love and leading to self-control (temperance). The Holy Spirit uses the Word of God to cultivate the soil of our lives so we produce this fruit.

Moreover, the Holy Spirit uses the Bible to produce stability (Psalm 1:1–3), to bring spiritual prosperity (Joshua 1:8) and to win others to Christ (Psalm 126:6).

The Children of Israel were instructed in the Old Testament to keep the Bible constantly before them and in them in order to show their faith in God. They hung it on their walls; they put it on their jewelry; they repeated it in their songs. It gave them a new look.

List the evidences in your life that you are growing spiritually.

_____

_____

_____

_____

_____

Lesson 2

The Believer and the Book

Passage to Reread: Psalm 119:1–24
Passage to Review: 2 Timothy 2:15

New Love

As we have seen in lesson 1, when the new life in Christ is nourished by the Word of God, it gives a new look to the believer. This process of development through the Word will also develop new loves. The values of the new life contrast sharply with the values of the old life (2 Corinthians 5:17). We should not be content to remain the same. Our priorities will change if we habitually study and obey God's Word.

Looking different does not mean we have to give up everything and lead boring lives in order to maintain the new look. We will not succeed by forcing ourselves to be "spiritual." Our motivations and desires will change as we grow spiritually. Initially we will be motivated by observing godly examples. Then as we study and obey God's Word, we will develop new loves that will motivate us inwardly; our desire will be to please God.

New Lifestyle

The Holy Spirit is our constant companion, called alongside us. He will also be our comforter. "For we know not what we should pray for as we ought: but the Spirit itself maketh intercession for us. . . . He maketh intercession for the saints according to the will of God" (Romans 8:26, 27).

The Spirit uses God's Word to nourish us; therefore, we must systematically read it daily for instruction (Hebrews 5:12–14). The Spirit will never tell us to do something that is contrary to the Bible (Psalm 119:105, 130).

We must memorize the Bible in order to have victory over the Devil. For example, Psalm 119:11 says, "Thy word have I hid in

10

mine heart, that I might not sin against thee." Similarly, Ephesians 6:11 and 17 command us, "Put on the whole armour of God, that ye may be able to stand against the wiles of the devil. . . . And take the helmet of salvation, and the sword of the Spirit, which is the word of God."

Our countenances (facial expressions) will be changed by the Spirit of God using the Word. We will know joy and fullness of life. "And he shall be like a tree planted by the rivers of water, that bringeth forth his fruit in his season; his leaf also shall not wither; and whatsoever he doeth shall prosper" (Psalm 1:3).

God's Spirit indwells us as tutor and companion; He has gifted and empowered us to communicate Christ to others. Communicating Christ becomes one of our new loves. Furthermore, we will enjoy the privilege of encouraging others (1 Corinthians 14:12).

Finally, the Bible warns us against hearing the Word of God and not obeying it (Ezekiel 33:23–33; Matthew 7:24–27). "But be ye doers of the word, and not hearers only, deceiving your own selves" (James 1:22).

What values have changed in your life since you became a

believer? _____

_____

_____

What new loves have come into your life? _____

_____

_____

Principles to Practice

1. **Use or copy the following chart to keep a record of your study of the Bible, memorization of Scripture, obedience to the Word and opportunities to witness.**

2. **Obtain your own copy of the Bible for personal study. Ask your pastor for (1) a list of good Bibles with accurate translations and helpful study guides; (2) the names of solid Chris-**

tian bookstores where you can obtain a Bible; and (3) a list of Bible versions to stay away from.

3. Seek a discipler to assist you in your Bible study. Again, ask your pastor's advice.

4. Choose a friend to witness to this week. Ask God to give you wisdom about when and how to present the gospel to that friend.

	Sun.	Mon.	Tues.	Wed.	Thurs.	Fri.	Sat.
Scripture Studied							
Application for Today							
Ways I Applied the Lesson							
Verse Memorized							
Person to Whom I Witnessed							

Prayer

Ask the Lord to give you understanding as you study the Bible. Commit your way to your growth and to obedience of the Bible. Ask God for the new look that is motivated by new loves. Confess the sins called to your attention by the Spirit of God through His Word (1 John 1:9).

Lesson 3

The Believer and the Bounty of Prayer

Passage to Read: Acts 4

1. Identify the following:

    a. The "they" in verse 1 _____

    b. The "they" in verse 3 _____

    c. The "many of them" in verse 4 _____

2. Why didn't the religious leaders punish Peter and John (vv.

14–17)? _____

3. What did the religious leaders command Peter and John

(v. 18)? _____

_____

_____

4. Study the believers' prayer in verses 24–30.

    a. In verse 24 they identified God and praised Him for

    _____ .

    b. In verses 25 and 26, they quoted _____ (Ps. 2:1, 2).

    c. In verse 27, they rehearsed _____ .

    d. In verse 28, they acknowledged God's sovereignty. What-
    ever happened occurred because God had planned it
    "_____ to be done."

    e. In verses 29 and 30, they asked God to give Peter and John
    _____ to speak God's Word and to do signs and
    wonders by Christ's name to authenticate their message.

13

5. What was the result of their prayer?

a. They spake the word of God _____(v. 31).

b. The apostles witnessed with _____(v. 33).

c. The believers shared their_____; there was unity among them (vv. 32, 34, 35).

Passage to Memorize: Luke 11:9 and 10

Introduction

"Prayer changes things." Perhaps even before you were saved, you saw this saying on a plaque, on a poster or even on a bumper sticker. Have you ever wondered, "Why, if prayer changes things, has so little changed? Thousands of prayers are offered daily, so why don't I see miracles right and left?"

The answers are simple: Not everyone who prays gets heard. And not everyone who gets heard is praying for the right things. And everyone who prays for the right things doesn't pray for the right reasons. Therefore, we need to note seven facts about prayer and the true purpose of prayer so our prayers will indeed change things.

What Is Prayer?

Before we accepted Christ as our Savior, most of us had misconceptions about prayer. Let's note seven facts about prayer.

First, prayer is hard work. It is not rote recitation such as, "Now I lay me down to sleep." Furthermore, it is to be our first course of action, not a last resort. If Satan can keep us from praying, he has kept us from a close walk with God and effective service for Him.

Second, prayer is a command (1 Thessalonians 5:17). From the divine perspective, God is sovereign and does as He wills. But for our benefit, He expects us to ask in order to receive (Luke 11:9, 10).

> When [we] pray, something happens which would not have happened if [we] had not prayed. . . . We are not trying to change God's mind or get Him to do something He doesn't want us to do. We are simply giving Him the opportunity to do for us what He most desires to do. (Clifford Richmond)

Third, prayer is a weapon, along with God's Word, against the evil forces that war against us.

> For we wrestle not against flesh and blood, but against principalities, against powers, against the rulers of the darkness of this world, against spiritual wickedness in high places. Wherefore take unto you the whole armour of God, that ye may be able to withstand in the evil day, and having done all, to stand. And take the helmet of salvation, and the sword of the Spirit, which is the word of God: praying always with all prayer and supplication in the Spirit, and watching thereunto with all perseverance and supplication for all saints (Ephesians 6:12, 13, 17, 18).

Fourth, prayer is power. Charles Haddon Spurgeon remarked, "The power of prayer can never be overrated. They who cannot serve God by preaching need not regret. If a man can but pray, he can do anything. He who knows how to overcome with God in prayer has Heaven and earth at his disposal."

It has been said that the great preacher George Whitefield could cry "oh," and conviction would sweep over the crowd. His greatest preparation for His sermons was prayer.

Fifth, prayer is the way to fruit bearing. Rachel's problem—barrenness—is our problem today. Her prayer must be our prayer, "Give me children, or else I die" (Genesis 30:1). John Knox prayed, "Lord, give me Scotland or I die!"

The New Testament church described in Acts chapter 4 was a growing, preaching, witnessing, praying church. The heathen raged like a wild, snorting stallion standing against the horizon. The religious court ruled that the church must stop preaching Christ. This satanic cry seems no different from the snorting of modern-day worldliness, rationalism and ritualism.

Sixth, prayer is a great privilege. Satan assails us. It is God's plan that the pressures of life bring perseverance and prayer (Romans 5:3–5). We must keep our eyes up so that our chins will stay up. Consequently, we need to exercise faith and give first place to prevailing (winning) power over temptation.

Seventh, prayer is the greatest resource. It gives the person in right relationship with God the ability to release God's power on earth and to achieve His purposes beyond human imagination. Note the results of the prayers of these Bible characters: Abraham withheld God's judgment from wicked Sodom for a time; Moses coped with a stubborn "church"; Jacob wrestled with God until He blessed him; the once-barren Hannah was given a child; Elijah controlled rain and fire; Joshua made the sun stand still; Paul and Silas brought an earthquake upon the jail.

> Prayer is the indication that God is stirring within us concerning some special need. . . . God puts us in tight spots to channel His creative faith through us. . . . When we pray we should say, "Lord, I am boldly interpreting this need as an evidence that you have the supply already on the way. I believe it. I receive it. Thank you." Then, if the supply doesn't come as we expect, whose business is it? Obviously His. Leave Him to mind His own business. (Norman Grubb)

When the company of believers in Acts 4 prayed, they did not ask for an easier place or life. They asked God for boldness with the result that "they [spoke] the Word of God with boldness" (v. 31). This account teaches us that prayer is the greatest resource of the church. Bent knees will bring blessing. This passage also demonstrates three principles of prayer that should operate in our lives:

• First, praise recognizes Who God is (Acts 4:23–28). The early Christians had the right perspective of sovereignty. They knew that God is the highest authority, the absolute ruler. Therefore, they gave the highest accountability to the Lord, not to human authority.

• Second, petition (asking God for things) recognizes what God can do (Acts 4:20, 30). The believers focused harmoniously on a common objective. Encouraged by God's sovereignty, they committed themselves to witness boldly to glorify the Lord (v. 29). Thus they experienced a direct answer (vv. 31, 33).

The plea of their prayer was for consistency. They gave themselves to God and trusted Him. Therefore, they did not ask for safety or peace. They cried for courage. They did not ask God to change the minds of the opposition; they did not ask for couches of ease or for a more convenient day and patience to wait. They asked for God's convicting power to convince the unsaved.

• Third, provision recognizes God's answer (Acts 4:31). The presence of the Holy Spirit among the believers was evident. The power of Pentecost continued as seen in the bold witness of the early Christians. It continued during oppression: further persecution resulted in further planting of churches (Acts 8:1).

Imagine receiving the news that you have inherited a vast estate of inestimable value. Funds have been deposited in the bank on which you may begin to draw. Checks that bear the signature of the authorized person have been given to you, thus giving you access to this vast wealth. The checkbook has no stubs since the deposits are unlimited. You can never overdraw. But you must write the checks and submit them—checks bearing the authorized signature.

That is prayer! God has made us joint heirs with Christ. He has given us all things to enjoy. We have the checks of prayer, which bear the signature of Christ. Prayer is writing a check on the Bank of Glory. God's bounty can be our blessing through prayer.

What Is the Purpose of Prayer?

You ask, "Why pray?" I answer, "Why write a check?"

The Bible says, "Call unto me, and I will answer thee, and shew thee great and mighty things, which thou knowest not" (Jeremiah 33:3).

Just as cashing a check is a prerequisite for receiving money, prayer is the prerequisite to spiritual blessing. "Ye lust, and have not: ye kill, and desire to have, and cannot obtain: ye fight and war, yet ye have not, because ye ask not" (James 4:2). All of our desires, appeals and efforts to obtain are futile apart from asking God.

Furthermore, God expects to be asked. "Thus saith the Lord God; I will yet for this be enquired of by the house of Israel, to do it for them; I will increase them with men like a flock" (Ezekiel 36:37). Accordingly, God expects several to ask for the same thing (Matthew 18:19).

Prayer is the means of praising God for blessing. Read the prayer found in Luke 11:1–4 that the Lord taught the disciples as instruction for prayer. "Our Father which art in heaven, Hallowed be thy name" acknowledges the Person of God as the Holy One of Heaven, the sovereign Who has the ability to solve problems and meet needs.

"Thy kingdom come. Thy will be done . . ." recognizes that it is God's purposes and plans that we are praising Him for. We surrender our selfish desires in order to praise God that He has a plan for history that includes us.

17

Prayer petitions God for blessings. Only God can bless us. Every believer in Christ has been made a priest with access to God through Christ our High Priest, Who is seated at the Father's right hand. His intercession for us is His primary task today (Matthew 7:7–11; Hebrews 4:14–16; 7:25; 1 Peter 2:9).

Read Philippians 4:6 and 19. Make a list of prayer burdens for which you will petition God until they become blessings through His answers.

BURDENS	BLESSINGS

Lesson 4

The Believer and the Bounty of Prayer

Passage to Reread: Acts 4
Passage to Review: Luke 11:9 and 10

The Purchaser in Prayer

Who is addressed in prayer? Since God the Father, God the Son and God the Spirit are equally God as the Trinity, should we give them equal time in our prayer ministry? "Holy Father . . . Precious Holy Spirit . . . Dear Lord Jesus"?

While this concept might make sense, it is not supported in the Word of God. For even though the three Persons of the Godhead are co-equal and co-eternal, the Bible teaches an agreed and distinct order of ministry among them. This is especially apparent in the New Testament in the teachings of Christ and the subsequent writings following His finished work on Calvary, which made our sonship a reality. Now we can call upon "our Father."

"And he said unto them, When ye pray, say, Our Father which art in heaven . . ." (Luke 11:2).

"And in that day ye shall ask me nothing. Verily, verily, I say unto you, Whatsoever ye shall ask the Father in my name, he will give it you" (John 16:23).

"Peter therefore was kept in prison: but prayer was made without ceasing of the church unto God for him" (Acts 12:5).

Since prayer is being viewed as writing a check on the Bank of Glory, who is authorized to sign the checks? Do I sign the check? No, I only send the check to the Father; it must bear the signature of Jesus Christ. We conclude our prayers "in Jesus' name" since it is only in His authority that we have access to the Father. Christ is the high priest of us believer-priests who come to His throne room. It is His merit that has established the account (John 14:13, 14; Philippians 4:19).

"If thou count me [Paul] therefore a partner, receive him [Onesimus] as myself. If he hath wronged thee, or oweth thee ought, put that on mine account" (Philemon 17, 18). This text describes the act of God in accounting righteousness to the believer in Christ. Christ bore the believer's sin and thereby provides access to the Father.

Our prayer checks are sent to the Father in the name of the Son. The Holy Spirit gives us the ability to pray correctly—to write the right checks. He ministers within us through the Word of God. Obviously, a right relationship to the Father through obedience to the Word is essential to the Holy Spirit's working in us for an effective prayer life (Romans 8:26, 27).

Summarize the principles you have learned in this section that

are the essentials of an effective prayer life: _____

_____

_____

The Program of Prayer

You ask, "When should I pray?" I answer, "How often may you write a check?"

There are many settings noted in the Bible for times of prayer. In Matthew 6:6 and 7 the Lord speaks of a time of private prayer to be viewed as intimate personal conversation with the Father:

> But thou, when thou prayest, enter into thy closet, and when thou has shut thy door, pray to the Father which is in secret; and thy Father which seeth in secret shall reward thee openly. But when ye pray, use not vain repetitions, as the heathen do: for they think that they shall be heard for their much speaking.

Unlike some people we have met in our human experiences, our Heavenly Father expects to be asked again and again. James 1:5 says, ". . . let him ask of God . . . that upbraideth not. . . ." The term "upbraideth not" means that God doesn't scold us for asking.

1. The best time for prayer and Bible study is when we are at

our best mentally and physically. **Find these references and indicate the time of day for prayer.**

   a. Mark 1:35—

   b. Luke 6:12—

2. **There are several illustrations of public prayer in the Bible. Find these references and indicate the unique features in each instance of prayer.**

   a. Matthew 18:19 and 20—

   b. Luke 19:46—

   c. John 17—

   d. Acts 1:14—

   e. Acts 2:42–47—

The Priorities of Prayer

How can we collect when we write a prayer check?

First, the Bible teaches that we must have proper attitudes when we pray.

3. **List the attitudes found in these passages.**

   a. James 5:16; Psalm 66:18—

   b. James 1:6; Mark 11:24; Romans 10:17—

   c. John 15:17; 1 John 3:21 and 22—

   d. Romans 8:27; James 4:15; 1 John 5:14 and 15—

   e. Luke 11:1–10; 1 Thessalonians 5:17—

   f. Philippians 4:6 and 7—

Second, praise to God should be a priority of our prayer lives according to Psalms 145 through 150. James 1:17 says that God is the giver of good. The glory belongs to Him.

Third, we are also taught in the Bible to give priority to asking specifically.

4. List the specific targets for petition found in these references.

    a.   James 1:5 and 6; Psalm 119:18—

    b.   Psalm 51—

    c.   Galatians 6:1 and 2; Ephesians 3:14–21; James 5:16—

    d.   Romans 10:1—

    e.   1 Timothy 2:1–6—

    f.   Psalm 122:6—

    g.   Matthew 9:38; Acts 13:2 and 3; Colossians 4:3—

    h.   Acts 14:23; 1 Thessalonians 5:12 and 13; 1 Timothy 5—

Although we may have the right priorities for prayer, our prayers may be hindered! What did we do wrong?

5. In these passages, find the reasons for unanswered prayers.

    a.   Isaiah 59:1 and 2—

    b.   James 4:3—

    c.   Proverbs 21:13; Philippians 4:14, 18, 19—

    d.   Mark 11:25—

e. 1 Peter 3:7—

f. Matthew 6:5—

g. James 1:5–7—

Principles to Practice

Based on the principles of prayer taught in this lesson, determine your personal daily prayer plan. State your plan. Make a prayer list for specific petitioning.

Prayer

Ask the Lord to teach you to pray. Admit that the time you are the busiest is the time you need to pray the most. Recognize that you have not adequately prepared for life's experiences until you have prayed. Commit yourself daily to praising and petitioning God. Expect your prayer burdens to become prayer blessings for which you will give God the glory.

Lesson 5

The Believer and the Beauty of Holiness

Passage to Read: 2 Peter 1

Choose the correct answer.

1. This letter was written by a(an) ____ to other ____.
   a. apostle, apostles
   b. pastor, pastors
   c. believer, believers
2. He wanted ____ and ____ increased in their lives.
   a. holiness, peace
   b. grace, peace
   c. faith, grace
3. Through the knowledge of Christ they received ____.
   a. precious promises
   b. forgiveness of sins
   c. earthly wisdom
4. Christ has called us to ____.
   a. witnessing and praying
   b. love and good works
   c. glory and virtue
5. Peter said they should diligently add virtue, knowledge, self-control, godliness, brotherly kindness, love and ____.
   a. generosity
   b. truthfulness
   c. patience
6. If a believer has these qualities, he will be ____ in the knowledge of Christ.
   a. fruitful
   b. unfruitful
   c. superior
7. Peter was writing to them to stir up their ____ (vv. 12–15).
   a. emotions
   b. memories
   c. talents

8. Peter and the other apostles did not teach ____ about Christ because they were ____ what really happened.
   a. everything, ignorant of
   b. speculations, realists about
   c. fables, eyewitnesses of
9. Peter heard God say about Christ, ____ (vv. 16–18).
   a. "Well done, thou good and faithful servant."
   b. "This is my beloved Son, in whom I am well pleased."
   c. "Thou shalt call his name Immanuel."
10. Prophecy of the Scripture has no ____interpretation.
   a. complete
   b. universal
   c. private
11. The prophecy came as men were ____.
   a. seeing visions
   b. discussing religion
   c. moved by the Holy Spirit

Passage to Memorize: Psalm 17:15

Introduction

In our modern world, the farmer may have graduated from the college of agriculture of one of the major universities. Perhaps he has inherited the family farm. He may also have the best equipment and experience along with his formal education.

The successful farmer knows when and how to prepare the soil. He is trained in the correct planting methods, and he uses the seed selections bred for his farm conditions. He fertilizes, sprays the appropriate weed killers and pesticides, cultivates twice and harvests with finely tuned machinery to save every grain. He knows when to market for the best prices.

Yet the Christian farmer has come to realize that farming is a joint venture between God and man (especially in times such as the drought of 1988). The farmer cannot do what God must do. Furthermore, God will not do what the farmer should do.

Some have called this principle the divine/human cooperative. It may be applied to all of life, including the believer's responsibility of holy living. Attaining holiness is a joint venture between God and the Christian. God has provided Christ to defeat sin and the Holy Spirit to empower us for victory. It is our responsibility to walk in holiness.

Often we reluctantly face our responsibilities. We pray for victory. But that is not enough. We must also obey the Word of God in order to become holy. That is our responsibility if our Christian lives are to be wholesome and happy.

We have been saved to live for Christ, to please God and not ourselves. Consider these Bible texts that teach the purpose of our lives and challenge us to the goal of holiness:

"Neither yield ye your members as instruments of unrighteousness unto sin: but yield yourselves unto God, as those that are alive from the dead, and your members as instruments of righteousness unto God" (Romans 6:13).

"There hath no temptation taken you but such as is common to man: but God is faithful, who will not suffer you to be tempted above that ye are able; but will with the temptation also make a way to escape, that ye may be able to bear it" (1 Corinthians 10:13).

A general rule of conduct for the believer is stated in Colossians 3:17, "And whatsoever ye do in word or deed, do all in the name of the Lord Jesus, giving thanks to God and the Father by him."

While the primary purpose of holy living is for our own good, we are challenged to this goal by the following truth: We are always being observed by others, and we must not cause them to stumble in their Christian walk because of our lifestyles. The angels also observe us. (See Ecclesiastes 5:6 and 1 Corinthians 4:9.)

We are told in Hebrews 12:14 to "Follow peace with all men, and holiness, without which no man shall see the Lord." The term "follow" means to chase or pursue. Thus the believer must make chasing holiness his occupation, one that requires diligence and effort. It is a life-long process; we will never fully attain holiness in this life. But it is the goal that we are to pursue diligently.

You can live a holy life. There is a Bible answer for your anger, temper, immoral conduct, defeat, enslaving habits and besetting sins. Holiness is the promised birthright expected of every believer (Romans 6:14).

The Command to Be Holy

In Leviticus 11:44 and 1 Peter 1:16 we are commanded, "Be ye holy; for I am holy." What is this Biblical command of holiness? Does it mean for a woman to wear bunned hair, long

26

sleeves and skirts and black stockings? Is it a "holier than thou" attitude because of our abstention from such things as smoking, drinking, cursing or dancing? No. Nevertheless some of these things should be evidences of holiness.

Or is holiness expressed in the receiving and exercising of special ecstatic "spiritual" gifts such as speaking in tongues, prophesying or divine healing? No, but every believer does have the indwelling Holy Spirit and is gifted to serve in a Biblical way that will develop His church.

The Biblical definition of holiness is to be morally blameless, separated from sin and consecrated to God. Theologian W. E. Vine has defined holiness as "separation to God, and the conduct befitting those so separated."

This holiness is more than "cultural holiness." We are not simply to adapt to the character and behavior patterns of the Christians around us (2 Corinthians 10:12). However, we are to conform to the character of God. Holiness is the result of our obedience to the Word of God rather than our practice of a list of external rules.

First John 1:5 says, "God is light, and in him is no darkness at all." Light is the absence of darkness. Similarly, holiness is the exclusion of all evil. God knows what is right, and He can do *only what is right*.

The command of holiness for the believer is a command to conform to Christ's divine character. We must mature in our Christian lives to make our thought lives (or knowledge of right according to the Bible) consistent with our actions.

When we are inconsistent, we disappoint ourselves. God always acts consistently and has called us to His standard. Healthy, normal Christianity conforms to the holiness of God in Christ. The psalmist gives us a prayer to pray constantly: "As for me, I will behold thy face in righteousness: I shall be satisfied, when I awake, with thy likeness" (Psalm 17:15).

The Contrasts of Holiness

How have New Testament writers used the word "holiness"? They often used it in contrast to those characteristics of the old life that are to be "put away." Let's examine a few of these pas-sages. For a better understanding of how the believer's life is to be different from the life of the worldling, notice the contrasts between the two.

In 1 Thessalonians 4:3–7, you will find the terms "sanctification" and "holiness." They come from the same basic word. Holiness is contrasted to a life of immorality and impurity.

12. List the contrasts of the old and new lives. Use a Bible dictionary or another translation of the Bible to understand what these terms mean. Ask for help if you need it.

    a. What is the contrast in Ephesians 4:22 and 24?

_____

    b. What is the contrast in 1 Peter 1:14–16?

_____

Holiness is not a condition of salvation. Our salvation does not depend on our attaining some level of personal holiness. Holiness is a part of salvation. The sinless Christ's finished work in dying for our sins gave each of us who have received Christ as Savior a permanent *standing* of holiness. "By the which will we are sanctified [made holy] through the offering of the body of Jesus Christ once for all" (Hebrews 10:10).

This standing is contrasted with our present *state*. Our position of holiness before God in Christ makes us strive for a state of holiness in daily practice. This is normal Christianity. (See 1 Thessalonians 4:7.)

The Character of Holiness

The Bible is a practical book; it is not just a list of teachings and commands. While commanding us to be holy, it also gives us the practical qualities that characterize a life of holiness. Our faith is to be the means of virtue (conformity in daily living to the standards of our faith).

List the evidences that you are adding the following characteristics to your faith.

Virtue (Moral excellence) _____

Knowledge _____

Temperance (Self-control) _____

Perseverance (Patience) _____

Godliness _____

Brotherly kindness _____

Christian love _____

Lesson 6

The Believer and the Beauty of Holiness

Passage to Reread: 2 Peter 1
Passage to Review: Psalm 17:15

The Conduct of Holiness

Why do we often feel defeated in our struggle with sin?

Perhaps our attitudes are self-centered rather than the way they should be—God-centered—so that He can teach us and direct our lives (Psalm 32:8).

Maybe we are more concerned with victory than with pleasing God and the truth that sin grieves the heart of God. Read David's confession in Psalm 51 and notice that it is addressed to God against Whom he had sinned. The prodigal son of Luke 15:11–24 learned that his defeat was due to a barrier in his relationship with his father. When he returned to his father, he found victory and the joy of obedience.

God wants us to walk in obedience to His Word (right actions toward Him). Then victory (holiness) will be a by-product of obedience (right actions toward ourselves).

It could be that we feel defeated because we have not become fully acquainted with what it means to live by faith. Paul said, "I am crucified with Christ: nevertheless I live; yet not I, but Christ liveth in me: and the life which I now live in the flesh I live by the faith of the Son of God, who loved me, and gave himself for me" (Galatians 2:20). This statement does not mean that we do not have to expend effort. We are personally responsible for our actions and obedience to the Word of God. We must want to master what is mastering us. We can if we want to—by faith.

Another reason for our defeat is that we are more concerned about acceptance among others than acceptance with God. We may not take sin seriously. Note Solomon's warning: "Take us the foxes, the little foxes, that spoil the vines: for our vines have tender grapes" (Song of Solomon 2:15). The farmer had to take seriously the intrusion of the foxes into his vineyard when the vines were laden with fruit, lest the fruit be destroyed.

Likewise, compromise on little issues leads to greater downfalls. Sin is sin because God's Word forbids it. If we are to live lives of holiness, we must not categorize sin. Do you strive to obey all civil laws? Do you have secret indulgences of reading, listening and looking that may be little foxes destroying the virtues of holiness?

List some areas you believe might be the "little foxes" that

cause defeat in your chase of holiness: _____

_____

_____

Let's study Romans 13:12–14: "The night is far spent, the day is at hand: let us therefore cast off the works of darkness, and let us put on the armour of light. Let us walk honestly, as in the day; not in rioting and drunkenness, not in chambering and wantonness, not in strife and envying. But put ye on the Lord Jesus Christ, and make not provision for the flesh, to fulfil the lusts thereof."

In this passage there are three steps to victory. They are the conduct of the believer who has made enjoying the beauty of holiness the goal of his life.

• *"Cast off the works of darkness"* (Romans 13:12). Read 1 John 2:15–17 and James 4:4. What amusements of the world are hindering your progress in spiritual growth?

Read 1 Corinthians 6:19 and 20 and 2 Corinthians 6:14 and 17. What sinful habits and practices are defiling your body, which is His temple?

• *Conduct yourself honestly* (Romans 13:13). Read this verse in another translation.

1. **Across from the words listed below** (used in the King James Version), **write the word from the other translation of Romans 13:13.**

a. Rioting—

b. Drunkenness—

c. Chambering—

d. Wantonness—

e. Strife—

f. Envying—

• *Cater to the Spirit, not to the flesh* (v. 14).

2. What are we to do according to Romans 8:13 and 14? _____

_____

3. List three key word commands we are to obey according to Colossians 3:1–5.
   a.
   b.
   c.

4. On Whom are we to keep our eyes according to Hebrews 12:1

and 2? _____

The Care of Holiness

Have you ever gone to the doctor when you were ill and been told that you had a virus? You ached all over, you had no energy, your ability to function was gone. The doctor probably told you to get plenty of rest and to drink lots of water and other fluids. Then he, no doubt, prescribed an antibiotic to combat the virus.

Sin in our lives may cause us to respond in a similar manner in the spiritual sense. David lists for us in Psalm 38 many of the symptoms in his life when he harbored unconfessed sin: no soundness (health, stability) in the flesh (vv. 3, 7); no rest (v. 3); wounds stink and corrupt (v. 5); troubled, bowed down, mourning (v. 6); feeble (v. 8); sore broken (v. 8); disquieted heart (v. 8); groaning (v. 9); panting heart (v. 10); failing strength (v. 10);

blindness or poor eyesight (v. 10); friends stay away (v. 11); enemies seek harm (v. 12); like the deaf and dumb (v. 13, 14); sorrow continually before him (v. 17).

Special care must be taken in our lives to prevent the world's viruses from robbing us of our spiritual joy and success in living obedient lives. Preventing the virus is far better than dealing with the illness.

The world system ruled by Satan hurls at us the viruses of tolerance that will cause spiritual defeat. But the Word's vaccination of temperance (self-control) will prevent these viruses from infecting us.

5. Let's list the viruses and then find the vaccinations in each of the passages.

- Secularism—Nothing is sacred.
  a. 1 Peter 1:13–15—

- Conformity—Don't be different.
  b. Matthew 5:48—

- Corruption—Nothing is immoral.
  c. 1 Peter 1:14—

- Indulgence—Why not?
  d. 1 Peter 2:9–12—

    1 Thessalonians 5:22—

- Tolerance—Maybe later.
  e. James 4:7—

- Enticement—Look!
  f. 1 Timothy 2:9—

- Liberation—Equality! Compete!
  g. 1 Timothy 2:11—

- Situation ethics—Nothing is wrong.
  h. Philippians 4:8—

- Salvation—By works.
  i. Ephesians 2:8–10—

Through the study of this lesson, have you been convicted by the Spirit of God concerning things in your life that are not pleasing to God? Are there areas of disobedience to the Word of God? What should you do? Try harder not to do them again?

No. First, you must identify the specific sins about which the Holy Spirit has convicted you. This is a personal matter between you and your Heavenly Father. Then, follow the plan of confession found in 1 John 1:9, which says, "If we confess our sins, he is faithful and just to forgive us our sins, and to cleanse us from all unrighteousness."

Now claim the promise of this text. Confession means that you have acknowledged to God that these things are sin and implies your commitment to forsake them in true repentance. You can again enjoy the fellowship with your Heavenly Father that you have with Him as His child.

MY SINS:

MY CONFESSION:

Principles to Practice

1. **Cultivate your habit of daily prayer and study of the Bible. It is the key to spiritual growth. Read Isaiah 40:31 and 2 Timothy 2:15.**

2. **Covet the mutual encouragement of fellow believers. Read Hebrews 10:25. (The term "exhort" means to encourage.)**

3. **Desire the will of God for your life (Romans 12:1, 2).**

4. **Seek to have a good testimony before men.**

Prayer

Thank the Father for the position of holiness you have been given in Christ. Declare a goal—to conform daily to the Word of God. Make a commitment to thank the Lord daily for your progress, to confess your sins quickly and to be satisfied in becoming like Christ.

Lesson 7

The Believer Beckoned to Serve

Passage to Read: Acts 9

**Circle T if the statement is true, F if it is false.
If it is false, correct it.**

T F 1. Saul went looking for Christians to imprison.

T F 2. Saul met Jesus on the road to Damascus.

T F 3. Jesus likened Saul to a rebellious animal when He said, "It is hard for thee to kick against the pricks."

T F 4. The sight of Jesus scared Saul and the men with him.

T F 5. Saul became blind.

T F 6. Saul stayed with Ananias until Judas came to heal him.

T F 7. After Saul was healed, he was baptized.

T F 8. Immediately Saul began preaching.

T F 9. The disciples, who did not trust Saul, wanted to kill him, but he escaped.

T F 10. Saul went from Damascus to Jerusalem to Caesarea to Tarsus.

T F 11. The churches multiplied in number and in strength and in the knowledge of the Lord.

T F 12. Paul healed a man sick of the palsy and raised Dorcas (Tabitha) from the dead.

T F 13. Dorcas was a wonderful woman who did good deeds for others.

T F 14. Many believed on the Lord because of the miracle performed on Dorcas.

T F 15. A tanner opened his home to an apostle.

Passage to Memorize: Romans 12:1 and 2

Introduction

Teenagers are bombarded with life-molding questions. I faced them as a young person. Who is going to be my life's companion? What is to be my vocation in life? Must I go to college? If so, where? Are all Christians called to full-time Christian service? How may we know if God wants us in His service? Does the mission field have a claim on our lives? Is there a special call of God to be a pastor or a missionary? Or does the Bible present missionary service as an option, perhaps just for a short time, without the necessity of lifelong commitment? Is everyone a missionary? What steps should we take to know the answers to these critical questions?

I have discovered that success from God's perspective is for me to know and do His will. I have also discovered that He does not intend to hide His will from me. He wants me to know! Furthermore, I have discovered that I never get old enough, or wise enough, to end my process of successive decisions concerning God's will and direction for my life. The steps continue until His upward call.

The matter of our career goals can be successfully resolved only in the context of the plan that God has for *each of our lives*. Success is much more than being a self-made person. For God does have a plan for each of us. Furthermore, He will enable us to achieve His plan. We will exercise faith when we place our feet forward to take the next step.

We must not think that we may be too old or too young to begin. Nor should we decide that we are too established in our present careers for God to call us. I have learned that every bit of my training and experience has been woven into God's unique pattern of ministry for my life. Nothing has been wasted. Each of us must be ready to obey God's leading, even if He calls us into missions.

"Missions" may be defined as "the local believing church seeking to win others to the Christian faith, especially through a group of selected workers called missionaries." True missions sees medicine or social work as a means of opening doors to share the gospel.

A "missionary" (from a Latin word) or "apostle" (from a Greek word) is one sent with a message.

Read Matthew 13:38. The field is the world. It is to be concurrently reached through the church's sowing the seed of God's

Word in Jerusalem (at home), Judaea (in the state), Samaria (in the country) and in the uttermost parts of the world (Acts 1:8).

God loves the world and sent His Son to die for the world of sinners (John 3:16). That provision of a substitute for sinners was sufficient for the whole world; it is made efficient to "whosoever" will put his faith in Jesus Christ. Therefore, this good news is to be taken to the world, which is lost (Matthew 28:19, 20).

Yes, Christ has made satisfaction for the world's sin. It is our responsibility to share this satisfaction for sin as the solution for man's need. We dare not be selfish. "And he is the propitiation for our sins: and not for ours only, but also for the sins of the whole world" (1 John 2:2). But are we called to do more than be witnesses of Christ by life and lip as Christians? Is the Lord calling us to make our life's work that of full-time missionaries? How can we know? There are three calls that we must distinguish.

Three Calls

• First, the *call of salvation* is extended to the whole world. "For God so loved the world, that he gave his only begotten Son, that whosoever believeth in him should not perish, but have everlasting life" (John 3:16).

"Look unto me, and be ye saved, all the ends of the earth: for I am God, and there is none else" (Isaiah 45:22).

It was this call of salvation that came to cultured, religious, educated, socially elite Saul on the road to Damascus (Acts 9). His conversion through responding to the calling Christ turned a despiser into a disciple, a destroyer into a devotee, an assailant into an apostle.

• Second, the *call to surrender* is extended to those who answer the call of salvation. We answer the call of surrender by inviting Christ to be the lord of our life. Making Him lord of our life means giving Him total control of it. This call and our answer to it follow our initial experience of sonship, or becoming God's children by the new birth.

I beseech you therefore, brethren, by the mercies of God, that ye present your bodies a living sacrifice, holy, acceptable unto God, which is your reasonable service. And be not conformed to this world: but be ye transformed by the renewing of your mind, that ye may prove what is that good, and acceptable, and perfect, will of God (Romans 12:1, 2).

Please notice that surrender involves the believer's entire being—body, intellect and will:

The body is to be presented in *separation*.

The intellect is to experience *transformation* of the mind renewed by the Word and the Spirit of God.

The will then yields to the perfect intention of God in respect to *occupation*.

• Third, the *call of special service* is extended by the Lord of the harvest (the Holy Spirit; see Matthew 9:38) to those He selects from among the surrendered to minister the Word of God. We have noticed in Romans 12:1 and 2 that we must be surrendered to God in order to know His will. This was the experience of Saul (later called Paul) according to Acts 9:15 and 16.

Paul recognized this special call of God in his life. His own testimony is recorded in 1 Timothy 1:12, "And I thank Christ Jesus our Lord, who hath enabled me, for that he counted me faithful, putting me into the ministry."

Following this call to minister the Word of God, Paul received directions from the Lord as to the geographical location and the means by which he was to minister. The call was to minister the Word; the directions related to location and methods within his occupation. During his ministry he served as a teacher, a pastor, a church-planter, a prisoner, a counselor and a writer as well as other roles. In fact, he initially supported himself as a tentmaker.

Not all believers are called to full-time service. However, all believers are called to a dedicated life. Furthermore, all dedicated believers must honestly consider these Biblical principles:

• A believer must be dedicated if he is to discern God's plan for him. The Lord has the authority and right to call. Read 1 Corinthians 6:19 and 20.

• The world is a harvest field that demands reapers (John 4:35).

• Love for Christ is expressed in willing surrender. Samuel said, "Speak LORD, for thy servant heareth" (1 Samuel 3:9).

Stepping-stones to Service

Read Psalm 37:23. The phrase "stepping-stones" suggests several principles. First, it suggests progress toward a goal—the course of ideas in action rather than stagnation. Second, steps encompass the smallest possible moves in the course of time, without impossible jumps, leaps and bounds. Third, steps give direction if they are continued in a planned pattern toward the destination. Fourth, steps encourage logical sequence: step one to step two if we are to be able to take steps three and four. Fifth, the word "stones" implies that God has prepared them. Bricks, on the other hand, are made with our hands. For example, in 1 Peter 2:5 the believer is called a lively (or living) stone: "Ye also, as lively stones, are built up a spiritual house, an holy priesthood, to offer up spiritual sacrifices, acceptable to God by Jesus Christ."

Which calls have you answered? Are you willing to answer the next one?

List the directions God has given you to serve. Are you obeying them? Across from each one, add the way you serve. (For example, "to usher"—Once a month I usher in three services.)

AREA OF SERVICE	MEANS OF SERVICE

Lesson 8

The Believer Beckoned to Serve

Passage to Reread: Acts 9
Passage to Review: Romans 12:1 and 2

Introduction

Early in my years of preparation for the ministry, I listened to a godly pastor, Dr. Reginald L. Matthews, as he presented "Stepping-stones to the Mission Field," based on the principle of Psalm 37:23, "The steps of a good man are ordered by the LORD: and he delighteth in his way." The steps he shared helped me tremendously in seeking the answers to my questions concerning God's will for my life. I want to list these steps and add my commentary to suggest how we may know whether the Lord of the harvest wants to send us forth as laborers into the harvest field. Obeying the Lord has been for me a far more rewarding path than wealth or fame.

Eight Steps to Special Service

Step One: Salvation

God is not going to send the Devil's children out to be ambassadors for Christ; He will send only His own children. How can a person become a child of God? According to John 1:12 those who believe on the Lord Jesus Christ have the authority to become the sons of God. A person can be saved by believing on the Lord Jesus Christ (Acts 16:30 and 31). At the Judgment Seat of Christ each of us children of God will give an account of what we have done with the gifts and opportunities given to us. (See 2 Corinthians 5:10.)

Step Two: Dedication

Read again Romans 12:1 and 2 and the previous section in lesson 7 concerning the calls of God to salvation, surrender and service. Have you taken this step of dedication? Do you need to renew your commitment? Without the step of dedication, you cannot know God's will for your life.

Step Three: Recognition

We also must recognize the role of the Bible in our lives. "Thy word is a lamp unto my feet, and a light unto my path" (Psalm 119:105).

God's authority in our lives is expressed through the Word of God. It tells us that God has a claim on our lives. "Know ye that the LORD he is God: it is he that hath made us, and not we ourselves; we are his people, and the sheep of his pasture" (Psalm 100:3).

1. **What phrases in this verse express God's claims that we must recognize?**

    a. Creative claim:

    b. Redemptive claim:

    c. Directive claim:

The Great Commission recorded in Matthew 28:19 and 20 recognizes the authority of God's Word and uses it to disciple individuals for Christ:

• First, *"Go ye therefore"* means that, based upon Biblical authority, you are to be involved for Christ, motivated by your recognition of this authority.

• Second, *"Teach all nations"* means to make disciples by teaching them the content of God's Word, which you have learned. Read 2 Timothy 2:2.

• Third, *"Baptizing them"* speaks of picturing their identification with Jesus Christ through salvation. We are to be baptized as obedient followers of Christ. Then we must seek to instruct other believers in this step of obedience. We must recognize and share this Bible message.

• Finally, *"Teaching them to observe all things"* is the Biblical method of instruction about Christ. As we study the New Testament instructions to the Church, we will recognize our responsibility to identify with a local church.

Step Four: Affiliation

If we are to become missionaries, we must be identified with the local church by membership. The visible local church is His means of spreading the gospel today (Acts 2:46, 47).

Believers have the responsibility of carrying out missionary work through local churches that honor God's Word. God recruits new missionaries from those disciples developed through the Word. They, in turn, establish new churches.

It is the local church that sends forth missionaries according to Acts 13:1–3. (Missionary agencies assist churches in this process of commissioning missionaries. Fundamental Baptist agencies require membership in a local church in order for a missionary to be sent through the agency.) Therefore, we must affiliate with a church that shares our convictions. The New Testament church always commissioned the missionary to go forth to duplicate his local church's convictions. Today we, too, must affiliate with a church that honors the Bible's teachings and practices. We want to support only missionaries who will reproduce our Biblical beliefs and convictions. And if we become missionaries, we want to duplicate the doctrine and practices of our supporting chruches.

Our most valuable preparation to be missionaries—if God calls us to special service—is our involvement in the ministries of the local church. First, we will learn to discipline ourselves to serve with accountability. Second, our pastors have been entrusted with the responsibility of equipping us to serve according to our gifts and abilities. By serving, we will be edified and will gain our pastors' valuable counsel regarding our future ministries. Third, the experience of learning to work with others on the team is essential preparation; it will prepare us to serve harmoniously with a group of missionaries and teach us how to equip our new church constituencies to serve. Our primary task in missions ultimately leads to church planting, which is similar to our present church experiences.

Step Five: Vision

"Say not ye, There are yet four months, and then cometh harvest? behold, I say unto you, Lift up your eyes, and look on the fields; for they are white already to harvest" (John 4:35).

The believer destined for a mission field of the world has a sense of urgency and vision concerning a world that is Hell-bound. He is personally involved now in activities similar to those of a missionary.

2. What are three of these activities according to the following passages?

        a. Matthew 9:38—

        b. 1 Corinthians 16:1 and 2—

        c. Acts 1:8—

First, the future missionary has a vision of the great need of the world. The world's population reached 5 billion in July 1987. Second, the future missionary has a vision of the great need of cities. The combined population of New York, Tokyo, Shanghai and Mexico City is 50 million people. There are more than 155 cities with a population in excess of 1 million. Third, he has an understanding of the growth of false religions. At present trends, by the year 2000 only 2 percent of the world will be nominally Protestant. Furthermore, he has a vision for his own country. The mission fields of the world are coming to America.

Do you have a vision for the lost? Determine to ask God regularly to send missionaries to _____(choose a field). Determine to witness to at least one person: This week I will witness to _____ as God gives me opportunity.

Step Six: Preparation

In Romans 1:15 Paul says, "So, as much as in me is, I am ready to preach the gospel to you that are at Rome also." If we have been called to special service, it is never too early to begin our preparation in order to be ready when candidate school and appointment time arrive (two early steps in becoming a missionary). The formal preparation of Bible school is totally inadequate if we have not disciplined ourselves in other areas of life prior to our formal training. In fact, the earlier disciplines are undoubtedly the most valuable preparations. What preparations are involved in being ready to serve?

Physical—We must give constant attention to good health. A physically strong missionary will be the most effective in ministry. We need to learn to eat the right foods in order never to have to discard bad habits. Each of us should learn to control his body weight now; as we get older, this task becomes more difficult. We need proper exercise and rest.

Mental—We must develop good personal study habits now. The disciplines of learning a new language and a new culture must be developed before we reach that responsibility. Bible college and seminary training demand the same study skills needed for other careers. We should learn to read and write well; we must know the content of Scripture and be able to communicate clearly in order to be effective missionaries.

3. Dedication involves good use of the mind. Read these passages of Scripture and summarize the responsibility for the mind in each:

   a. Romans 12:2—

   b. Philippians 4:4–8—

   c. 2 Timothy 2:15—

Spiritual—We can gain spiritual discernment through exercising (training) our senses. We will not lead people to a level of spiritual maturity beyond that which we ourselves have attained. These texts are not optional for the believer:

"But grow in grace, and in the knowledge of our Lord and Saviour Jesus Christ" (2 Peter 3:18).

"But strong meat belongeth to them that are of full age, even those who by reason of use have their senses exercised to discern both good and evil" (Hebrews 5:14).

We must do more than read a two-minute daily devotional and listen to our pastors' sermons. We have to read the Bible. Furthermore, we should develop our own study libraries. We need to discipline ourselves to study the Bible systematically. The more we learn prior to our formal training, the more foundation we will have to build upon for that formal training and future ministry. We should be ministering now to develop the discipline essential for learning when we are in Bible school.

Social—Each of us must choose the right life's mate. That person should be a believer who is committed to doing God's will. Our mates should share our Biblical convictions. Furthermore, our life's partner must support our call to minister the Word. Otherwise, we will probably never be able to fulfill God's will for our lives.

Furthermore, we all must learn to get along with people. To do so we must overcome a self-centered attitude. We need to orient ourselves to encouraging others and building them up. We must also learn to forgive. We should become good listeners. We can study the materials of good Christian writers regarding relationships and put the principles into practice in our lives now. It will be too late when we are thrust into the missionary field council (a support group that works together).

Financial—Now is the time to learn to live within our means. We can avoid debt by operating our personal lives on a cash basis. We should study materials related to personal finances. We must budget our expenditures and live within our budgets. We should tithe our incomes and entrust all that we have to the Lord; we must be acceptable to Him. We should maintain reasonable lifestyles so we do not have to make drastic changes when we become missionaries. It is wise for us to save money for education, retirement and other proper goals. We cannot go to the mission field while owing debts. Furthermore, we cannot borrow money to live on the mission field.

Formal—We can seek counsel from our pastors, missionaries, Baptist college personnel and mission personnel in order to choose a proper place to train for our work. We should value the counsel of the experienced and let them direct us into training that will be adequate for the ministry in which we will be involved. Others may have greater knowledge and experience to direct us within God's will for us.

Step Seven: Information

Information creates interest. It can be used of the Lord to confirm our call to minister the Word as well as to give us direction to the area of ministry that is in God's plan for our lives.

We should listen to those who are already serving and spend time with missionaries whenever possible. The more we read, the more we'll learn. We should learn what the requirements are in each field of the world, not just the one in which we have an interest. We ought to develop our world vision through information. If possible, we should visit mission fields. Furthermore, we can contact Baptist mission agencies and express our interest and desires.

Step Eight: Faith

God's will is known and achieved one step at a time. "God gives His best to those who leave the choice to Him." This step does not require a sacrifice if the other steps we have taken have led to a commitment to know success by God's definition—to know and to do the will of God. We will have to sacrifice personal fulfillment and joy only if we seek to live *outside* the will of God.

Where do *you* need to begin? What is *your* next step?

Principles to Practice

1. **Publicly dedicate yourself to do whatever God asks you to do in order to demonstrate that you have surrendered your will to Him.**

2. **Witness to one person this week as a result of your love for the Lord and your vision for the lost.**

3. **Add this prayer burden to your prayer list: ask the Lord to send missionaries to specific countries and peoples.**

4. **Write to or pick up information about a mission agency.**

5. **Read one missionary biography this month.**

6. **Join a missionary support group.**

Prayer

Acknowledge God's claim on your life. Surrender your will to His lordship. Tell God that you are willing to be what He wants to make of you even though you recognize your inadequacy for the task apart from His enabling.

Commit yourself to die daily to selfish ambitions and desires. Be willing to take the steps outlined in this lesson, and let the Lord open and close the doors.

Lesson 9

The Believer
and Betrothal for Life

Passage to Read: Luke 19:1–10

There is a children's song based on this passage. Match the phrase of the song with the verse from which it is taken.

1. Zacchaeus was a wee little man, and a wee little man was he. v.____

2. He climbed up in a sycamore tree, for the Lord he wanted to see. v.____

3. And as the Savior passed that way, He looked up in the tree. v.____

4. And he said, "Zacchaeus, you come down." v.____

5. "For I'm going to your house today, for I'm going to your house today." v.____

Passage to Memorize: 2 Timothy 2:2

Introduction

Have you ever noticed on the wall of someone's home a plaque that says, "Christ is the head of this house, the unseen guest at every meal"? If our homes are to be pictures of the relationship of Christ and the Church, the effects of His presence must be visible in them. Christ said to Zacchaeus, "I must abide at thy house" (Luke 19:5). Christ must be a permanent resident in our homes if our marriage relationships as Christians are to be successful as God counts success. How may we make Him at home in our houses?

• **Invite Him in!** Luke 19:6 indicates that Zacchaeus joyfully received Christ. His must be a personal entrance by the new birth, which is subsequently followed by a deliberate beginning and continuous action to bring Christ in (Revelation 3:20).

The application of the principle of Revelation 3:20 is not just for us to adopt a set of standards. Christ is a real person, not just an ethic (system of moral values). We must constantly be aware of His abiding presence to know the joy of His peace and comfort. He must be more than an occasional guest. (See Hebrews 4:13.)

• **Introduce Him to your family!** "This day is salvation come to this house . . ." (Luke 19:9). The Bible teaches the necessity of each individual receiving Christ in order to become His child. The individual salvation of each person in a home is seen in Acts 16:30–34 in a setting of rejoicing as the entire household had come to personal faith in Christ.

The salvation of the parents will not save the children. God has no grandchildren. However, the godly saved parents will endeavor to live Christ and to lead the children to salvation in Him. (See 2 Timothy 3:15.)

• **Inaugurate Him as controller of the house!** When Christ came to the house of Zacchaeus, the tax collector said, "Behold, Lord, the half of my goods I give to the poor; and if I have taken any thing from any man by false accusation, I restore him four-fold" (Luke 19:8).

Christ is the One Who will never leave us and Who will stand with us in every trial. He is the Holy One Who seeks to influence our actions. We must surrender control of our homes to Him to know His power for peace and joy. We must deliberately say, "What would Christ want me to do?" and then do it. Labor must be service for Him.

Which of these is true of your home?

_____ Christ is the head of this house.

_____ The children are the head of this house.

_____ The parents are the head of this house.

_____ Circumstances are the head of this house.

• **Involve Him in every action!** We have unlimited potential for blessing if we make Christ part of every activity. We will honor Him with the topics of conversation at the table, claim the promises of His care for the family, acknowledge His presence and praise Him in prayer, ask Him to help us perform each task, and ponder His Word to seek His direction. He will be the source of purity and godliness, which lead to true happiness.

Is Christ in control of your home? Do you have disciplined television viewing habits? Are you discerning in your radio listening? Is your selection of literature discreet? Is there delightful conversation between husband and wife, between parents and children and even among the children? The clearest mark of His presence is love: "By this shall all men know that ye are my disciples, if ye have love one to another" (John 13:35).

Do you enjoy this kind of home? Or is Christ knocking at the door waiting for you to let Him in to be the center of your life? Are you cultivating those qualities that make a happy Christian home?

Let's examine several passages of Scripture to learn how God has planned for us to be equipped for marriage and the Christian home.

The Foundation of the Home

The foundation for home life must be built early. It is never too early to begin preparing for marriage. "For as [a man] thinketh in his heart, so is he" (Proverbs 23:7). This foundation for a home must be built upon the Word of God so that the person thinks right: "For other foundation can no man lay than that is laid, which is Jesus Christ" (1 Corinthians 3:11). The Bible indicates three essential building stones that must be laid successively for a Christian home.

An Adequate Person

The first stone is an **adequate person,** a believer who is saintly in a life separated to God. We are now becoming what we are going to be. Until we develop adequately as persons, we are not equipped for partnership or parenting.

List proper habits that you will practice in order to keep your body strong, healthy and revealing your best appearance:

_____

_____

_____

An adequate person is strong in mind. We should make it our goal to develop our maximum intellectual potential. We must seriously use our educational opportunities. Furthermore, we need to follow the principles for the mind taught in Philippians 4:8 and 9. We should think about things that are true, honest, just, pure, lovely, of good report, virtuous and full of praise.

An adequate person is strong in spirit. Strong Christian character is essential to strong Christian relationships.

6. What are the products of being strong in the Spirit according to Galatians 5:22–24? _____

_____

7. What principles are we to practice from Galatians 6:7–9?

_____

_____

An Adequate Partner

The second foundation stone for a Christian home is an **adequate partner.** Each of us must be an adequate person before we can be an adequate partner. Then, each of us must follow God's directions in the Bible to choose that person who is best suited for being our adequate partner. The person equipped for partnership is a saint who is willing to practice a life of self-sacrifice.

The Bible addresses the question of how to choose one's partner for life. "Can two walk together, except they be agreed?" (Amos 3:3). The more points at which two lines find common ground, the stronger the relationship. The partnership is strong when the same interests are involved, whether they be fishing, flowers or finances.

Similar backgrounds are important, especially in respect to economic levels, education, social preferences, family lifestyles and race. Moreover, the same faith is crucial. "Be ye not un-equally yoked together with unbelievers: for what fellowship hath righteousness with unrighteousness? and what communion hath light with darkness?" (2 Corinthians 6:14). This text teaches a principle of similarity. It should be understood to teach that both partners should be saved; both should come from the same kind of church; both should be church workers.

List points about yourself that you want to make common ground with your life's partner so that you can have a strong relationship: _____

_____

An Adequate Parent

The third foundation stone for a truly Christian home is an **adequate parent.** This is a separated saint (adequate person) who has learned to be a sacrificing saint (adequate partner) and is now willing to be a serving saint (adequate parent). Only then can a married couple properly assume the responsibilities of parenting.

"Train up a child in the way he should go: and when he is old, he will not depart from it" (Proverbs 22:6). The term "train" is from the word for palate. In Old Testament times, the midwife massaged the roof of a baby's mouth with dates in order to induce sucking and appetite. She endeavored to create a taste for food. Parents are to train their children—to create a taste for the things of God. This term is used in the Bible with children of every age.

"Way" in this text means "his way." The term comes from the original root meaning of "bending the bow." Each child has his own unique makeup, talents, gifts and personality. It is the parents' responsibility to train each of their children in a manner that will lead each child to reach his own potential.

"Old" speaks of hair or fuzz on the chin—the teen moving on to maturity and making his own decisions. It is the parents' awesome task to equip the child—through teaching by word and example—to reach his full potential, honoring the Lord with his lifestyle and choices as he assumes responsibility for his life. Only mature parents can lead their children to maturity.

If you are a parent, how are you training your children? State the method(s).

By your example—

By teaching them Scripture—

By not frustrating them—

By rebuking them when they are wrong—

51

Lesson 10

The Believer and Betrothal for Life

Passage to Reread: Luke 19:1–10
Passage to Review: 2 Timothy 2:2

Introduction

Noah was a successful father when the rest of the world was wicked and continually evil (Genesis 6:5). He reared his three sons to follow him in obedience to God in spite of the world's ridicule. He helped them find, out of this wicked world, partners who joined them in honoring God.

We are not going to find the ideal environment in this sin-cursed world unless we create it in our own homes. We have the responsibility in our homes to develop a lifestyle and culture that are patterned after the Bible's principles rather than the world's mold. That responsibility means we must make daily choices that are based upon the Word of God rather than on peer pressure or other influences.

Characteristics of the Home

The early pioneer family was a symbol of strength, courage, faith, love and unity. Few modern families know the hardships and simplicity of that day. Yet the need for character and spirituality in family life has not changed with the changing times. A Christian home must be more than a shelter from storms and cold, a place to be fed and a place to sleep. We raise hogs that way. Child rearing entails the building of Christian character in order to make the Christian home a great influence for God and good.

The Christian home conforms to the will of God according to the Word of God. Therefore, the Bible must be read daily, discussed as a family and practiced diligently. The Christian home is a home delighted with Christ; consequently it is filled with the

Spirit of God. Its goals are built around the question, "What would Christ have us do?"

The spiritual and material standards taught in Scripture and practiced by the Church should be duplicated in the Christian home. If they are, the parents will desire to please Christ in order to produce Christlike character in their children. The result of Christlike character is love, which quickly resolves the normal strains of human relationships.

In addition, the Christian home is challenged to meet the church's needs. We must never let our children hear us criticize the pastor or church. We have to instill a sympathetic interest in church life and teach our children good church habits. Good character is caught as well as taught.

The Head of the Home

Men and women have respective places in God's order. The beautiful picture of the Christian home in Ephesians 5:21–33 reveals a place of mutual love, devotion and respect. God's plan for marriage can be fulfilled only by ardent believers.

Galatians 3:28 teaches that all believers are one in Christ. While equality and unity are to be noted, God has also established organizational laws to help the home function properly. For example, Christ is a model of lordship and love.

1. **The husband is to be head of the household. What does this involve?**

    a. What is the husband's relationship to his wife according to

    1 Corinthians 11:3? _____

    b. Does this make his wife his slave or hired servant? _____

    _____

    c. What is the man's responsibility to the woman according to

    Ephesians 5:25–28? _____

    d. What is man instructed to do in Deuteronomy 6:6–9 and

    11:18–21? _____

    _____

e. What is the man to do according to 1 Timothy 3:4? _____

_____

f. What is the warning of Proverbs 29:15? _____

_____

The Bible teaches us aspects of lordship for the husband to practice:
• Christ is responsible for our needs (Philippians 4:19), and the husband must meet his family's needs.
• The husband is responsible for the supplies to accomplish the duties of each family member. Look at 1 Timothy 5:8.

The husband's primary role in lordship outlined for us in the Bible is that of a spiritual leader. He teaches the wife and family by his example the spiritual responsibilities of praying, studying the Bible, tithing, obeying the law, attending church, godly living and acting responsibly. The husband should not expect the privileges of lordship without assuming the responsibilities.

The head of the house follows Christ's example in lordship. He is also to follow Christ's example of loving. He cultivates love relationships that become stronger and better, rather than wane (decrease) with the years. He seeks to satisfy others' needs, whether those needs are physical, emotional, mental, cultural or spiritual. His wife's slightest need is his greatest desire to fulfill.

Our home lives set the pattern for our children's future homes. Do we have Christian homes? Are we making them Christ-centered in character? Do they meet the challenge of today's needs? Does the husband provide a Christlike model for his family? Do *your* children have a godly example to follow in establishing their homes?

The Helper of the Home

God has given the woman an exalted position as a woman, wife, mother and homemaker. First, she need not mimic or compete with men to seek a position of honor by usurping the man's role. Second, she is not an object. Among pagan peoples, women are degraded as slaves to be bought and sold. The gospel delivers women to a position of honor and respect. Third, the Hollywood model of women is not the Bible's model. So where do we find our heroines?

A woman is at her best fulfilling God's purposes for her. Let's

54

examine the three purposes that relate to the Christian home.

First, she is privileged to be a wife. God designed the woman to be man's suitable helper (Genesis 2:20–25).

2. She is to stand with her husband in every phase of life.

a. What kind of helper is she in Ephesians 5:22? _____

_____

b. What may she expect in return according to Ephesians 5:25?

_____

c. What traits are noted of godly wives in 1 Timothy 3:11? ____

_____

Second, the woman of God has power as a mother. God has suited her psychologically for motherhood. Motherhood should be sought as a sacred privilege.

3. A mother has power as a spiritual tutor.

a. What is the mother's role in 2 Timothy 3:15? _____

_____

b. What opportunity does a Christian mother have according

to 1 Corinthians 7:14? _____

_____

Third, the woman has a high calling in her performance as a homemaker. Homemaking is a ministry of love. The housewife does not labor out of fear or duty. Her work is never drudgery even though it is sometimes boring and seems never to be done.

4. The Bible makes the homemaker much more than a domestic worker.

a. How is her homemaking viewed by God in 1 Timothy 5:14

and 15? _____

b. While the husband is the head of the house, who has the vital delegated administrative role according to Proverbs 31:27? _____

_____

"A prudent wife is from the Lᴏʀᴅ" (Proverbs 19:14). Home-making is the highest of careers; it should have precedence over all other careers. A spiritual mother will make her husband great (Proverbs 31:23), and she will be praised (Proverbs 31:30).

Principles to Practice

1. Review lesson 9 (pp. 47–51). List your physical weaknesses. Next to each one that you can change, write a plan of action to change it. Carry out your plan. At the end of this course, return to this page to check on yourself. Have you carried out your plan? How close are you to reaching your goal?

2. After reviewing lesson 9, list the things that you can do to improve yourself intellectually. Be careful not to set impossibly high goals. Keep in mind the time and money you have available.

3. Outline a plan for spiritual growth. Include nourishment and exercise:
   Nourishment
   • appetizers (Scripture reading)
   • main meal (Bible study)
   • dessert (Scripture memorization)
   • snacks (meditation)

   Exercise
   • warm-ups (attendance of church and Sunday School)
   • regular routine (witnessing; stewardship of finances and time)
   • aerobics (exercise of spiritual gifts)
   • cool down (attendance of special meetings and conferences)
   • individual sports (witnessing, stewardship)
   • team sports (visitation, stewardship, spiritual gifts, service)

4. You listed the things you would like to have in common with your spouse. Plan a strategy to develop these common interests.

5. Make a two-column list of your strengths and weaknesses as a spouse. Decide what to do to improve in your weak areas and to maintain your strengths.

6. If you are a parent or a child still under your parents' authority, make a two-column list of your weaknesses and strengths as a parent or child. Decide how to make improvements and to maintain good qualities.

7. Believe that marriage is for life and do everything in your power to remain happily married.

Prayer

Ask the Lord to give you courage to do whatever is necessary to fulfill your responsibility in allowing God to make you what He has intended you to be. Begin with being an adequate person. Then sacrifice selfish ambition to be an adequate partner if God gives you that privilege. Finally, should the Lord entrust children to your care, give them back to Him and commit yourself to rearing them in the fear and admonition of the Lord.

Lesson 11

The Believer and the Blessed Hope

Passage to Read: John 14:1–6

1. Fill in the blanks.

Christ told His disciples "Do not let your hearts be troubled. Trust in God; trust also in (a)_____" (John 14:1, NIV). In God's house are many (b)_____ . Christ left earth to (c)_____ a place for believers. He promised, (d)"_____

_____" (John 14:3, KJV). (e)_____ did not understand Christ's words. Christ then declared that He is the (f)_____, the (g)_____ and the (h)_____ and that no one can go to the Father except by Him.

Passage to Memorize: John 14:3

Introduction

What does your future hold for you? Life is filled with uncertainties from the human perspective. Nevertheless, we Bible Christians can have confidence that we will spend eternity with our Heavenly Father in the dwelling places that Christ is preparing for us. This is our blessed hope: "Looking for that blessed hope, and the glorious appearing of the great God and our Saviour Jesus Christ; who gave himself for us, that he might redeem us from all iniquity, and purify unto himself a peculiar people, zealous of good works" (Titus 2:13, 14).

This blessed hope that Christ will call us Home to be with Him may happen today. Our eternal destiny with Christ has been guaranteed by our personal faith in Christ as Savior. The Rapture (snatching away) of the believers of the Church Age will end our earthly pilgrimage, taking us to our citizenship in Heaven where we will be changed to be like Christ in glorified bodies and to live with Him forever (Philippians 3:20, 21).

This anticipated call Home, accompanied by the resurrection of all who have died in Christ, motivates us to live right today.

> Behold, what manner of love the Father hath bestowed upon us, that we should be called the sons of God: therefore the world knoweth us not, because it knew him not. Beloved, now are we the sons of God, and it doth not yet appear what we shall be: but we know that, when he shall appear, we shall be like him; for we shall see him as he is. And every man that hath this hope in him purifieth himself, even as he is pure (1 John 3:1–3).

Our hope also motivates us to zealous service for Christ in preparation for standing before the Judgment Seat of Christ to be judged for our service. "Wherefore we labour, that, whether present or absent, we may be accepted of him. For we must all appear before the judgment seat of Christ; that every one may receive the things done in his body, according to that he hath done, whether it be good or bad" (2 Corinthians 5:9, 10).

Our sins were judged at the cross of Christ. Therefore, this judgment seat for believers pertains to the receiving of crowns for faithful service. Christ's judgment of our works determines whether they have worth or are merely wood, hay and stubble to be burned (1 Corinthians 3:12–15).

But how do we know about the Rapture, the Judgment Seat of Christ and other future events? Prophecy. Biblical prophecy foretells the future.

Duty of the Prophet

Prophecy was given by godly men who were led by the Holy Spirit (2 Peter 1:21).

> [The Old Testament] prophets were men raised up by God in times of declension and apostasy in Israel. They were

primarily revivalists and patriots, speaking on behalf of God to the heart and conscience of the nation. The prophetic messages have a twofold character: first, that which was local and for the prophet's time; and secondly, that which was predictive of the divine purpose in the future. Often the prediction springs immediately from the local circumstances (e.g., Isa. 7:1–11 with vs. 12–14) (*The Scofield Reference Bible* [New York: Oxford University Press, 1967], p. 711).

Definition of Prophecy

The Bible prophets spoke the message of God to the people. Theirs was not a message merely to eliminate curiosity concerning the future. They stated the message they had received to people who were then challenged to act on the basis of the information given.

God used chosen men to be His spokesmen to other men for the purpose of speaking His truth. A portion of this truth was predictive; it gave new information concerning the future. God could predict the future with complete accuracy since He is the planner and controller of all events. Therefore, the prophet's voice was really God's voice. It was a voice of authority pleading with men to return to God. Predictive prophecy prompts faith in God.

Some of these proclaimers and foretellers of God's truth were commissioned by God to write this truth into what became our Bible. It is comprised of sixty-six books written by about forty different human writers over a period of fifteen hundred years. Their ministry of writing the Word of God may be called inscripturation—the communication of God's truth in words so that the message might be preserved and accurately communicated until all of the message is fulfilled.

God gave these prophets special miracle-working powers so that He could demonstrate to their listeners that the prophets were true messengers from God and that their message was God's message. Now that the Bible is complete, we are warned not to add to the message or to take anything away from the Bible (Revelation 22:18, 19). Furthermore, we believe that the purpose for these sign miracles has passed now that the Bible has been completed.

Therefore, we may conclude that there are no true prophets today since God's message to us is complete in the Bible. Any miraculous deed would not be for the purpose of authenticating

God's messenger since we have the Bible to test each spokes-man's message. If it agrees with the Bible, it is true. If it adds to the Bible, it is false since we are told that God's message in the Bible is all we need for today.

Difficulty in Interpreting Prophecy

Prophecy is perhaps one of the most difficult areas of inter-pretation for several reasons:

• The content of Scripture on future things is deeply complex with many details and problems of correlation.

• Prophetic utterances often involve imagery and symbols. Future events are revealed also through types, parables, dreams and prophetic ecstasy as well as through straightforward proph-ecy.

• Things near to and far from the writer are mixed. Events that are separated in fulfillment by many years or ages may be compounded (predicted as if they were to occur at the same time or close in time).

• Men cause confusion by their failure to adhere to a consis-tent Biblical system of interpretation. This gives rise to different schemes of prophecy. They interpret most of the Bible teaching literally, but turn to allegorizing in the doctrinal areas of the Church and the subject of last things (eschatology). They also improperly apply the literal/cultural/critical principles of inter-pretation to specific passages, resulting in errors.

Differences in Interpreting Prophecy

There are two basic errors that give rise to these different schemes of prophecy.

• The **Rapture** is confused with the **Second Coming.** The rapture of the church is not preceded by signs while the second coming of Christ, primarily for Israel, must be preceded by signs prophesied by Christ Himself, most of which will occur during the Tribulation.

• God's program for **Israel** is confused with the program of God for the **Church.** The Church is a mystery, not found in the Old Testament prophecies, but revealed in the age after Israel rejected the Messiah. (Look at Ephesians 3:1–13.) Israel still has a literal earthly future concerning God's promises. The Church has not replaced Israel in God's program.

The Distinctions of Prophecy

Three distinct identities are described for us in 1 Corinthians 10:32, "Give none offence, neither to the Jews, nor to the Gentiles, nor to the church of God."

The Jews (Israel) are God's earthly people to whom *Christ is presented as a king.* The promises concerning this chosen nation were given to Abraham.

2. Read Genesis 12:1–3. List the promises you find in this passage.

    a. _____

    b. _____

    c. _____

3. The family covenant with the Jews is still to be fulfilled according to Romans 9—11. What will happen to Israel according to Romans 11:23? _____

_____

The Gentiles (nations) are seen in the Bible in relation to God's chosen nation, the Jews. *Christ is presented to the Gentiles as judge.* Daniel gives us the framework for all prophecy and defines for us the "times of the Gentiles," which is controlled by God. Most of the prophecies for the Gentiles have been fulfilled. Gentile rule is doomed. God will soon judge the nations for their unbelief and in relation to their treatment of the Jewish nation.

The Church is God's heavenly people to whom *Christ is lord.* The Church, the Body of Christ, was pictured in the Old Testament by God's chosen earthly people, Israel. It was predicted by Christ in Matthew 16 and born at Pentecost in Acts 2. The Church becomes functional in the Book of Acts and in the Epistles. It is consummated in the prophecy of Revelation 2 and 3.

Christ could come to rapture (snatch away) the Church at any moment. Are you ready? If not, what things in your life need to be changed? List them. Across from each one, write your plan of action.

NEEDS	PLAN

Lesson 12

The Believer
and the Blessed Hope

Passage to Reread: John 14:1–6
Passage to Review: John 14:3

Delights of Applied Prophecy

The large volume of prophecy in the Bible should be viewed as a great source of encouragement and strength. Seventeen books of the Old Testament are classified as prophecy. In addition, portions of Genesis, Deuteronomy, the Psalms and 1 and 2 Kings are prophetic.

The New Testament contains a large volume of prophetic content. The parables of Matthew and chapter 24 speak of Christ the king presented to Israel, with practical value for the church. Luke 21, Acts 15:14–18, 1 Corinthians 15, 1 and 2 Thessalonians, 1 and 2 Peter, Jude and Revelation offer volumes of information concerning the future upon which the Bible believer can build great hope—an assured Christian expectation.

There are dangers to be avoided that come from false approaches to prophecy and lead to speculation rather than interpretation.

The **fanatic** compares every false leader to the Antichrist, predicting dates and gathering with others on haystacks to wait for the Rapture.

The **dogmatic** makes interpretations and identifications of prophetic truth based on current events rather than on Bible truth.

The **indifferent** says eschatology is unimportant; he does not read it, saying it cannot be understood.

The **rationalist** makes human reasoning and logic the key to all prophetic truth. He shows literalness as being unreasonable.

The enemies of prophecy are apparent. They deny prophetic truth as expected according to 2 Peter 3:4, "And saying, Where is the promise of his coming? for since the fathers fell asleep, all things continue as they were from the beginning of the creation."

These basic rules of interpretation will guide us to a practical knowledge of prophetic truth upon which we can base our present life and future hope:

• Interpret literally, understanding there may be figures of speech. But if the literal makes sense, seek no other sense.

• Interpret according to the harmony of prophecy, interpreting the obscure in light of the obvious.

• Observe the perspective of prophecy, researching the background and purpose of the writer, as well as the people addressed.

• Observe the time relationships of events.

• Interpret prophecy Christologically, knowing that all prophecy focuses on revealing Christ in all His glory, honor and power.

• Interpret according to history and grammar, not violating either.

• Interpret according to the law of double reference since many prophetic utterances may have an early, as well as later, fulfillment in relation to events concerning Israel.

• Interpret consistently.

Declaration of Prophecy

Christ is coming! The prophets have foretold it.

> Immediately after the tribulation of those days shall the sun be darkened, and the moon shall not give her light, and the stars shall fall from heaven, and the powers of the heavens shall be shaken: And then shall appear the sign of the Son of man in heaven: and then shall all the tribes of the earth mourn, and they shall see the Son of man coming in the clouds of heaven with power and great glory. And he shall send his angels with a great sound of a trumpet, and they shall gather together his elect from the four winds, from one end of heaven to the other (Matthew 24:29–31).

Many predictions of prophecy have been fulfilled:

• Daniel's image of Gentile nations has been fulfilled with the history of the Babylonian, Medo-Persian, Greek and Roman empires.

• Christ has come in humility—His human birth (Isaiah

7:14), the suffering servant (Isaiah 53) and the Messiah (Psalm 16:8–10).
   • Israel rejected Christ and is being prepared for regathering.
   • The Church was born and empowered but has become cold.

Unfulfilled predictions are to be fulfilled:
   • The glory of Christ will follow (1 Peter 1:10, 11).
   • The Church will be raptured (John 14:3; 1 Thessalonians 4:13–18).
   • The Tribulation will last seven years (Matthew 24:15, 21).
   • Israel will be regathered (Isaiah; Ezekiel).

The preparations are underway as foretold by Christ in John 14:1–6. His work on earth was completed in His death, burial, resurrection and ascension.

1. The work in Heaven is now underway.

   a. What is Christ doing according to Romans 8:34? _____

   _____

   b. What are His activities listed in John 14:1–3? _____

   _____

The work of Christ on earth is next. The stage is now being set! The following list of seven events are in chronological order according to literal interpretation of prophetic Bible truth. It is very important that you memorize these events in order as a framework for the study of future events. Locate each of the events on the chart that is provided with this study (p. 69).
   • RAPTURE accompanied by the first resurrection and rewards
   • REVEALING of the Antichrist after the rapture of the Church
   • RETRIBUTION for the sin of Israel in the Great Tribulation
   • RETURN of Christ with the saints to the Battle of Armageddon
   • REIGN of Christ for 1000 years (Millennium) on earth
   • RETRIBUTION for all revolters and rebels with the doom of Satan, second resurrection, Great White Throne Judgment, Lake of Fire
   • RECONSTRUCTION of new Heaven and earth

This plan may be enacted today, beginning with the sudden snatching away of the true believing Church.

2. What do the following references tell us about the Rapture?

    a. 1 Thessalonians 4:17—

    b. 1 Corinthians 15:52—

    c. Revelation 3:3—

    d. 2 Thessalonians 2:10–12—

3. The important practical lesson concerning this truth is preparation. What preparations are indicated in these passages?

    a. Ecclesiastes 12:1—

    b. 2 Corinthians 6:2—

    c. Romans 13:11–14—

    d. 1 John 3:1–3—

Principles to Practice

1. Each time you hear a preacher, speaker or televangelist, compare what he says with Scripture. If he's taking something out of context or adding to or deleting from Scripture, do not listen to him again. The same principle is true for authors. If you have questions, ask your pastor or another spiritual leader.

2. In referring to the Rapture, do not allude to characteristics of the Second Coming and vice versa.

3. Keep a balanced perspective of prophecy. Do not get stuck on a tangent.

4. Live a pure life because Christ may return in the air at any moment. Don't be ashamed when He calls.

Prayer

Tell the Father you believe the Bible is truth to be obeyed. Tell Him that you expect Christ to come at any moment. Thank Him for this blessed hope. Renew your commitment to "put ye on the Lord Jesus Christ, and make not provision for the flesh, to fulfil the lusts thereof" (Romans 13:14).

Things to Come

John 16:13

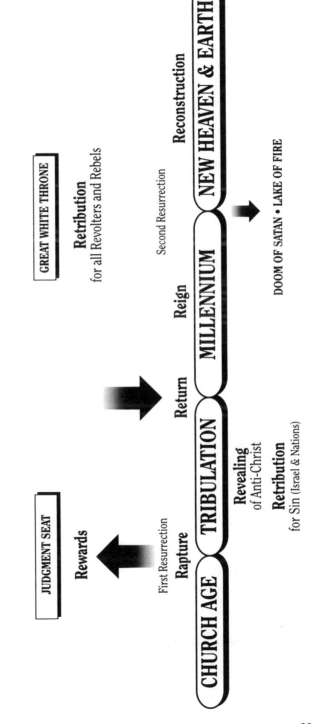

CHURCH AGE — TRIBULATION — MILLENNIUM — NEW HEAVEN & EARTH

JUDGMENT SEAT
Rewards

Rapture
First Resurrection

TRIBULATION
Revealing of Anti-Christ
Retribution for Sin (Israel & Nations)

Return

Reign

GREAT WHITE THRONE
Retribution for all Revolters and Rebels

Second Resurrection

Reconstruction

DOOM OF SATAN • LAKE OF FIRE

Answer Key

Lesson 1
The Believer and the Book

1. Verses	Name	Condition	Result
(a) 1, 18	law; law of the Lord	walk in the law of the Lord; undefiled	blessed
(b) 2, 14, 22	testimonies	keep His testimonies; seek Him with a whole heart	blessed
(c) 4, 15	precepts	respect all His commandments	
(d) 5, 8, 12, 16, 23	statutes	delight in all His commandments; meditate on them	
(e) 6, 19	commandments	respect all His commandments	shall not be ashamed
(f) 7, 13, 20, 21	thy righteous judgments	have learned and declared thy righteous judgments	praise God
(g) 9	thy word	take heed to thy word	cleanse my way
(h) 21	thy commandments	err from His commandments	rebuked; cursed

2. List the action words that tell what a Christian should do with God's Word.

a. walk in (1, 3)
b. keep (2, 4, 5, 8, 17, 22)
c. respect (6)
d. learn (7)
e. take heed to (9)
f. not wander from (10)

g. hide in the heart (11)
h. declare (13)
i. rejoice about (14)
j. meditate on (15, 23)
k. delight in (16, 24)
l. forget not (16)

Lesson 3
The Believer and the Bounty of Prayer

  1. a. John and Peter
     b. priests, temple leaders, Sadducees
     c. the people (v. 1) who heard Peter and John

2. They could not deny the miracle performed by Peter and John because a multitude saw it.

3. "not to speak at all nor teach in the name of Jesus"

4. a. His creation
   b. Scripture (Ps. 2:1, 2)
   c. history
   d. before
   e. boldness

5. a. with boldness (v. 31)
   b. great power (v. 33)
   c. material possessions (vv. 32–35)

Lesson 4
The Believer and the Bounty of Prayer

1. a. Mark 1:35—morning
   b. Luke 6:12—night

2. a. Matthew 18:19 and 20—Two or three are united in prayer; God is in their midst; God does what they ask.
   b. Luke 19:46—The worship center is characterized by prayer.
   c. John 17—Christ is praying for Christians.
   d. Acts 1:14—The men and women prayed with unity.
   e. Acts 2:42–47—unique unity; abundant growth

3. a. James 5:16; Psalm 66:18—with confessed sin, a desire for a clean heart
   b. James 1:6; Mark 11:24; Romans 10:17—believing, trusting
   c. John 15:17; 1 John 3:21 and 22—obedient, loving
   d. Romans 8:27; James 4:15; 1 John 5:14 and 15—submitted to God's will
   e. Luke 11:1–10; 1 Thess. 5:17—diligently, consistently
   f. Philippians 4:6 and 7—thankfully

4. a. James 1:5 and 6; Psalm 119:18—for wisdom; for understanding
   b. Psalm 51—for restoration
   c. Galatians 6:1 and 2; Ephesians 3:14–21; James 5:16—for a fallen brother; for each other

d. Romans 10:1—for lost Israel

e. 1 Timothy 2:1–6—for rulers

f. Psalm 122:6—for the peace of Jerusalem (Christ's return and eventual reign)

g. Matthew 9:38; Acts 13:2 and 3; Colossians 4:3—for missionaries

h. Acts 14:23; 1 Thessalonians 5:12 and 13; 1 Timothy 5—for spiritual leaders, pastors

5. a. Isaiah 59:1 and 2—You sinned.

b. James 4:3—You asked "amiss"; i.e., for the wrong thing or for the wrong reason.

c. Proverbs 21:13; Philippians 4:14, 18 and 19—You ignored others' needs; you're asking for a "want" instead of a need.

d. Mark 11:25—You have not forgiven others.

e. 1 Peter 3:7—You have a broken relationship with your spouse.

f. Matthew 6:5—You pray for show, to be praised by man.

g. James 1:5–7—You do not pray in faith.

Lesson 5
The Believer and the Beauty of Holiness

1. c. believer, believers
2. b. grace, peace
3. a. precious promises
4. c. glory and virtue
5. c. patience
6. a. fruitful
7. b. memories
8. c. fables, eyewitnesses of
9. b. "This is my beloved Son, in whom I am well pleased."
10. c. private
11. c. moved by the Holy Spirit
12. a. The old nature (man) before I was saved is contrasted with my new nature now that I have believed. The old nature was corrupt; the new nature is righteous and holy.

b. The old lifestyle (according to lust) is contrasted to the new lifestyle of holiness.

Lesson 6
The Believer and the Beauty of Holiness

1. a. Rioting—orgies; carousing; revelry
   b. Drunkenness—the condition of being drunk with alcohol (a condition in which control of the faculties is impaired and inhibitions are broken)
   c. Chambering—Sexual immorality; sexual promiscuity; licentiousness
   d. Wantonness—debauchery; sensuality; lewdness
   e. Strife—dissension
   f. Envying—jealousy

2. Mortify (to subdue or deaden) the deeds of the body.

3. a. Seek the things above.
   b. Set your affection on heavenly things.
   c. Subdue your body parts.

4. Jesus, the author and finisher of our faith.

5. a. 1 Peter 1:13–15—Be holy like the holy God.
   b. Matthew 5:48—Be like the Heavenly Father–perfection.
   c. 1 Peter 1:14—Be obedient to God's Word.
   d. 1 Peter 2:9–12—Abstain from fleshly lusts; do good works.
      1 Thessalonians 5:22—Don't even *appear* to do wrong.
   e. James 4:7—Submit to God; resist the Devil.
   f. 1 Timothy 2:9—Be modest.
   g. 1 Timothy 2:11—Be submissive.
   h. Philippians 4:8—Don't even *think* about bad things; think on honest, clean things.
   i. Ephesians 2:8–10—Believe, don't work for salvation.

Lesson 7
The Believer Beckoned to Serve

T 1. Saul went looking for Christians to imprison.
T 2. Saul met Jesus on the road to Damascus.
T 3. Jesus likened Saul to a rebellious animal when He said, "It is hard for thee to kick against the pricks."

F 4. The sight of Jesus scared Saul and the men with him. *Only Saul saw Jesus.*

T 5. Saul became blind.

F 6. Saul stayed with Ananias until Judas came to heal him. *Saul stayed with Judas until Ananias came to heal him.*

T 7. After Saul was healed, he was baptized.

T 8. Immediately Saul began preaching.

F 9. The disciples, who did not trust Saul, wanted to kill him, but he escaped. *The Jews wanted to kill him because he was an excellent preacher.*

T 10. Saul went from Damascus to Jerusalem to Caesarea to Tarsus.

T 11. The churches multiplied in number and in strength and in knowledge of the Lord.

F 12. Paul healed a man sick of the palsy and raised Dorcas (Tabitha) from the dead. *Peter healed . . .*

T 13. Dorcas was a wonderful woman who did good deeds for others.

T 14. Many believed on the Lord because of the miracle performed on Dorcas.

T 15. A layman opened his home to an apostle.

Lesson 8
The Believer Beckoned to Serve

1. a. Creative claim: "it is he that hath made us"
   b. Redemptive claim: "we are his people"
   c. Directive claim: "we are . . . the sheep of his pasture"

2. a. Matthew 9:38—praying for God to send missionaries
   b. 1 Corinthians 16:1 and 2—giving through the local church
   c. Acts 1:8—witnessing wherever I am

3. a. Romans 12:2—Renew it.
   b. Philippians 4:4–8—Rejoice; don't worry; think on good things.
   c. 2 Timothy 2:15—Study the Word of God.

Lesson 9
The Believer and Betrothal for Life

1. verses 2, 3
2. verse 4
3. verse 5
4. verse 5
5. verse 5

6. Love, joy, peace, longsuffering, gentleness, goodness, faith, meekness and self-control

7. a. God knows what we're doing (even if no one else does).
   b. What we sow (do), we reap (experience the result of); therefore, we need to sow to the Spirit (obey the commands of the Spirit).
   c. We should not become tired in well doing.
   d. We will be rewarded if we don't give up.

Lesson 10
The Believer and the Betrothal for Life

1. a. He is her head.
   b. No.
   c. He is an example and a leader, and he must treat her as Christ treats His own.
   d. First, man should know God's Word himself. Then he should teach it to and talk about it with his children. He should also display it.
   e. He is to rule his house well.
   f. An undisciplined child brings shame to his parents.

2. a. She is to be a submissive helper.
   b. She can expect her husband's self-sacrificing love.
   c. They are grave, sober and faithful. They are not slanderers.

3. a. She is to teach the Scripture and plan of salvation to her children.
   b. Her opportunity is to lead her children to holiness.

4. a. It is a testimony for Him against Satan.
   b. The wife has the role.

Lesson 11
The Believer and the Blessed Hope

1. a. me
   b. mansions
   c. prepare
   d. "I will come again, and receive you unto myself; that where I am, there ye may be also."
   e. Thomas
   f. Way
   g. Truth
   h. Life

2. a. "I will make of thee a great nation" (v. 2).
   b. "I will bless thee, and make thy name great; and thou shalt be a blessing" (v. 2).
   c. "I will bless them that bless thee, and curse [them] that curseth thee" (v. 3).

3. If they believe, they'll be grafted in.

Lesson 12
The Believer and the Blessed Hope

1. a. He is making intercession for us at the Father's right hand.
   b. He is preparing a place for us; then He will return for us.

2. a. 1 Thessalonians 4:17—"caught up together with them in the clouds to meet the Lord in the air"
   b. 1 Corinthians 15:52—"in the twinkling of an eye"
   c. Revelation 3:3—"as a thief"
   d. 2 Thessalonians 2:10–12—"strong delusion, that they [unbelievers left on earth] should believe a lie"

3. a. Ecclesiastes 12:1—Remember God during your youth.
   b. 2 Corinthians 6:2—Now is the time to prepare.
   c. Romans 13:11–14—Cast off the works of darkness; put on the armor of light; walk honestly; put on the Lord; make no provision for the flesh.
   d. 1 John 3:1–3—Look forward to Christ's return.